D1577230

REACHER'S
RULES

Jack Reacher, of no fixed address, is a former Major in the US Military Police. Since leaving the Army, the authorities have not been able to locate his whereabouts, although his name mysteriously crops up from time to time in connection with investigations into murders, terrorist threats and other breaches of the law.

www.leechild.com

REACHER'S
RULES

LIFE LESSONS FROM
JACK REACHER

With a foreword by
LEE CHILD

BANTAM PRESS

LONDON · TORONTO · SYDNEY · AUCKLAND · JOHANNESBURG

TRANSWORLD PUBLISHERS
61–63 Uxbridge Road, London W5 5SA
A Random House Group Company
www.transworldbooks.co.uk

First published in Great Britain
in 2012 by Bantam Press
an imprint of Transworld Publishers

Compiled by Val Hudson
Designed by Nick Avery Design
Original research by Dot Youngs

Photographs courtesy of Shutterstock.

A CIP catalogue record for this book
is available from the British Library.

ISBN 9780593070734

Addresses for Random House Group Ltd companies outside the UK
can be found at: www.randomhouse.co.uk
The Random House Group Ltd Reg. No. 954009

The Random House Group Limited supports the Forest Stewardship Council (FSC®), the leading
international forest-certification organization. Our books carrying the FSC label are printed on
FSC®-certified paper. FSC is the only forest-certification scheme endorsed by the leading
environmental organizations, including Greenpeace. Our paper procurement policy can be
found at www.randomhouse.co.uk/environment.

Typeset in Frutiger
Printed and bound by Clays Ltd, St Ives plc

2 4 6 8 10 9 7 5 3 1

MIX
Paper from
responsible sources
FSC® C016897

CONTENTS

'I'm a man with a rule. People leave me alone, I leave them alone. If they don't, I don't.'

REACHER'S
RULES

FOREWORD

If you've been paying attention long enough, you know one thing for sure: the defining human characteristic is tribalism. We all slice and dice the world's population into ever smaller fragments until we find a group where we feel comfortable, where we feel we truly belong.

And having arrived there, we make rules governing that group's behaviour. We want a reliable guide to how to act, we want to build bulwarks against outsiders, we want to provide a secure mechanism for belonging, we want to reassure ourselves that continuing membership is guaranteed if only we conform.

Some rules are official. We form clubs and societies and associations and give them procedures and by-laws more complex than government bodies.

Some rules are only semi-official. Hit on your friend's best girl? No way. Rat out an accomplice? Not going to happen. Break a strike? You'd rather die.

Some rules are just slogans, consoling and emboldening. Maybe as a kid, your gang – part of your street in part of your city in your country in the big, bewildering world – were, like kids are, told by your parents and teachers to be scared of strangers. No, you said. Strangers should be told to be scared of us.

Reacher has always followed his own rules. He grew up in a fractured way, six months here, three months there, always moving, never stable, never belonging. Then he was a soldier, but too wise to buy into all the nonsense. He only obeyed the rules that made sense to him. Then he was cut loose and became a true outsider, profoundly comfortable with solitude. Does he have a tribe? You bet. He's human. But in his case he kept on slicing and dicing until he got all the way down to a tribe with just one member – himself. But that tribe still needed rules, to guide, and embolden, and simplify, and reassure.

What follows are some of them.

LEE CHILD

BE PREPARED

'Hope for the best, plan for the worst.'

- Never count on anything except surprise and unpredictability and danger

- Ring doorbells with your knuckles or elbows to avoid leaving fingerprints

- Sit in diners or bars with your back to the wall so you cannot be surprised from behind

- Keep all exits in view

- Walk up the edge of stairs to minimize the chances of loud creaks. Stairs squeak at their centres where they're weakest

- Go to bed fully clothed so you are always ready for action

- Never look through spy holes in doors. Someone could be on the other side waiting to see the glass darken and shoot you in the eye

'We're making an omelette here … we're going to have to break some eggs.'

'Optimism is good. Blind faith is not.'

- Always lift a door handle upwards. If a door squeaks it's because it's dropped on its hinges. Upward pressure helps

- Climb through a hole feet first. If there's an axe or a bullet waiting, better to take it in the legs than the head

- If someone's likely to shoot at you, plant yourself in the middle of a restaurant full of people

'Most guys who don't check new equipment are still alive, but by no means all of them.'

- Never trust a weapon you haven't personally test-fired

- Before you use a car to commit a crime, get it cleaned thoroughly, inside and out, twice, to make sure you leave no DNA

- Always have a penny in your pocket, you never know when you're going to need it to unscrew a pair of licence plates

- If you are climbing up towards a trapdoor into an uncertain situation, catapult yourself up the last eighteen feet as fast as you can

'The less I relax, the luckier I get.'

THINGS YOU'LL NEVER HEAR REACHER SAY

Sorry, I've forgotten my watch.

BREAKING
AND
ENTERING

First thing to do before attacking a lock is to check it's not already open. Nothing will make you feel stupider than picking a lock that's not locked.

The bigger and more ornate the lock, the easier it is to pick.

'Get a problem, solve a problem.'

Iron bars protecting a window can be forced open with a tyre iron. Force it into the siding next to one of the screws. Make a shallow dent in the metal, shove the iron in sideways and under the bars, and haul on it until it gives.

For a door with a glass panel, use the sole of your shoe to break a hole in the glass, then reach through to the handle.

To kick a door down: take a run towards the door, making sure to stay upright, and with your dominant leg kick the area below the doorknob hard, using your sole or your heel.

(NB: All these techniques are most successful when there's no one home.)

CHOOSE
YOUR
WEAPONS

'A magazine he knew to be full, in a gun he knew to be working. A sensible step for a man who planned to live through the next five minutes.'

- Next to a shotgun, a pool cue is the best weapon in a fight

- A handgun at two hundred feet is the same thing as crossing your fingers and making a wish

- No point in having a weapon at all unless it's ready for instant use

- Don't trust a .38 calibre revolver. You can't rely on them to put a guy down

- A chisel plunged into the back of your head is going to seriously ruin your day

>>HOW TO USE A CIGARETTE AS AN EFFECTIVE
WEAPON

Take quick deep pulls to heat the coal on the end of the
cigarette up to a couple of thousand degrees. When it has
lengthened to a point like an arrow, apply quickly to a
vulnerable part of the body. Such as an eye.

- Rolls of quarters in your fist – good old-
  fashioned technology

- Choose the weapon you know for sure is in
  working order

- The longer a barrel the straighter it shoots

- A cup of hot coffee is also a weapon in the right
  hands

'Twelve-gauge lead shot settles most disputes at the first time of asking.'

- The best place to get hold of a random
  untraceable gun is to steal it from someone who
  already stole it. That way there are no official
  comebacks

- Keep a gun with a single shell locked in the chamber and all the other bullets loose. More jams are caused by tired magazine springs than any other single reason

>>CREATING A WEAPON FROM A CERAMIC BATHROOM TILE

Sharpen it into the shape of a knife. A bathroom tile, being entirely ceramic, is harder than anything except a diamond. Harder than steel, sharper than steel. And it won't trigger a metal detector.

THINGS YOU'LL NEVER SEE REACHER DO

Fill in an insurance form

★ ★ ★ ★ ★ ★

THE UNITED STATES ARMY
MILITARY POLICE

Law-enforcement branch of the United States Army, established to:

- maintain discipline and security in the army
- protect supply routes and guard prisoners
- act as a fighting force in combat
- act as peacekeepers at war's end
- aid disaster relief
- manage internal security
- uphold democracy

It is one of the most deployed branches of the Army.

'I don't come from anywhere. I come from a place called Military.'

MPs are also known as 'Snowdrops'.

The United States Army Military Police were given the affectionate nickname 'Snowdrops' by British soldiers and civilians during the Second World War. It came from their white helmets.

MPs are also sometimes less affectionately called 'Chimps' (Completely Hopeless in Most Policing Situations).

ASSIST, PROTECT, DEFEND

★ ★ ★ ★ ★ ★

THE RULES
OF COFFEE

'If in doubt, drink coffee.'

- Nothing's too urgent for coffee

- A bad coffee mug has a thick lip – too wide, too shallow, too much mass, it will cool the drink too fast

- A good coffee mug is cylindrical in shape, narrow in relation to its height and with a thin lip

'I love coffee. Give me the chance and I drink coffee like an alcoholic drinks vodka.'

'Coffee tastes better if the latrines are dug downstream from an encampment.'
US Army Field Regulations, 1861

'The Reacher brothers' need for caffeine made heroin addiction look like a little take-it-or-leave-it sideline.'

- Ignore the fancy brews and get a tall house blend, black, no cream

- It's all about the caffeine

- Coffee keeps you awake. Until you want to go to sleep

- Never say no to a cup of coffee

THINGS YOU'LL NEVER HEAR REACHER SAY

No more coffee for me

>>FIVE FACTS ABOUT COFFEE

1. The earliest recorded evidence of coffee drinking was in the middle of the 15th century in the Yemen

2. Drinking coffee increases short-term recall, and decreases the risk of gout in men over the age of forty

3. After petroleum, coffee is the second most traded product in the world

4. In North America and Europe the quantity of coffee drunk is about a third of that of tap water

5. Finland consumes more coffee per head than any other country

CONQUER YOUR FEAR

'I'm not scared of anybody ... But certainly I preferred it when he was dead.'

- Some things are worth being afraid of. And some things are not

- To be afraid of a survivable thing is irrational

- Focus on the job in hand

> *'Reacher didn't like crowds. He was a mild agoraphobic – from agora, the Greek word for a crowded public marketplace. Random crowds ... organized crowds ... riots and revolutions. A crowd is like the largest animal on earth – the heaviest, the hardest to control, the hardest to stop.'*

- A courageous guy is someone who feels the fear but conquers it

'Why are you going back?' 'Because they told me not to.'

'Sometimes if you want to know if the stove is hot the only way to find out is to touch it.'

- Try not to get trapped in the dark in close tight spaces

> *'He was a guy who survived most things, and he was a guy who was rarely afraid. But he had known since his early boyhood that he was terrified of being trapped in the dark in a space too small to turn his giant frame. All his damp childhood nightmares had been about being closed into tight spaces.'*

- Confront your enemies

- Take things exactly as they come, for exactly what they are

- Analyse your fear, it's probably not rational

- Turn your fear into aggression

'You see something scary, you should stand up and step toward it, not away from it. Instinctively, reflexively, in a raging fury.'

THINGS YOU'LL NEVER HEAR REACHER SAY

My knees are trembling and my hands are shaking

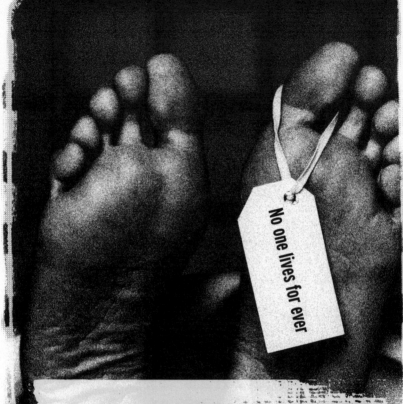

No one lives for ever

CONFRONTING
DEATH

'I'm not afraid of death, death's afraid of me.'

• It's a part of life, missing the dead

'People live and then they die, and as long as they do both things properly there's nothing much to regret.'

• Life's a bitch and then you die

• Soldiers contemplate death. They live with it, they accept it. They expect it. But deep down they want it to be *fair*

> *'In his head Reacher had always known he would die. Every human does. But in his heart he had never really imagined it.'*

• The meaning of life is that it ends

CRACKING
CODES AND
PASSWORDS

- Get into their minds, think like them

- Try birthdays, wedding anniversaries, house numbers, these are the passwords most people use

- Most people can't remember all their passwords. If you look, you can find where they've written them down

- Try two-digit prime numbers, or the number whose square root is the sum of its digits

- Watch the position of their fingers when keying in a code so you can copy them

The perfect PIN:

'I'd probably write out my birthday, month, day, year, and find the nearest prime number. Actually that would be a problem, because there would be two equally close, one exactly seven less and one exactly seven more. So I guess I'd use the square root instead, rounded to three decimal places. Ignore the decimal point, that would give me six numbers, all different.'

'Passwords come from down deep.'

DOGS

'I like dogs. If I lived anywhere I'd have three or four.'

- Don't leave dogs out overnight in a place where there are mountain lions. That's a sure way of having no dogs in the morning

- Remember dogs are different from people, no free will, easily misled. But on reflection – not *that* different

'You don't buy a dog and bark yourself.'

- Never show fear when facing fighting dogs

- Don't run away from dogs, walk

- Dogs trained to attack will attack anything that moves – including you

- When confronted by two or more dogs, be aware that like people, dogs have a pecking order. Two dogs, one of them has to be superior to the other, and will attack first

- You can intimidate a dog and show him who's boss by baring your teeth

FIGHTING

'You don't throw my friends out of helicopters and live to tell the tale.'

- Hit early, hit hard

- Stand with your back to the sun so that it's in your enemy's eyes

- Make the first shot count

- Get your retaliation in first – show them who they're dealing with

- Say you'll count to three – then throw your punch at two

- Never revive a guy who has just pulled a gun on you

- Train yourself to use aggression in the face of danger

'Soon as he was neutralized, it was two against one. And I've never had a problem with those kind of odds.'

- When confronted by two or more opponents, know that the one who does all the talking is the leader. Hit them first and hit them hard then the others will think twice

- Cheat. The gentlemen who behaved decently aren't there to train anybody. They are already dead

'Then I cheated. Instead of counting three I headbutted him full in the face.'

- If Plan A doesn't work, move on to Plan B

- If you have to fight five guys then identify the ringleader. Any five guys will have one ringleader, two enthusiastic followers, and two reluctant followers. Put the ringleader down, and both of the keen sidekicks, and it's over. The reluctant pair just run for it. It never gets worse than three-on-one

'Attacking me was like pushing open a forbidden door. What waited on the other side was his problem.'

- Look at each opponent in turn. Serene self-confidence works wonders

- Try not to get into a fight when you've just put on clean clothes

- Stay alive, and see what the next minute brings

- Never get distracted from the job in hand

- Use the first precious second for the first precious blow. Fight, and win. Fight, and win

- Don't think ahead – if you think about the aftermath you usually don't get that far

'His eyes were closed, which made it not much of a fair fight, but those are always my favourite kind.'

- Look like you mean it, and people back off a lot

FIGHTING TIPS

- -

✪ When you pull the gun, from that point on it's all or nothing

✪ The best fights are the ones you don't have

✪ Be on your feet and ready

✪ Assess and evaluate

✪ Show them what they're messing with

✪ Identify the ringleader

✪ Act, don't react

✪ Never back off

✪ Don't break the furniture

'He had no prejudice against fast food. Better than slow food, for a travelling man.'

- Don't eat before you go into an army post-mortem

- You need protein and fats and sugars, it doesn't matter where they come from

- Eat when you can because you never know when you will next get the chance

- Be friendly with the cookhouse detail

'I'm a big guy ... I need nutrition.'

- Eat and plan

- Always eat a perfect breakfast: pancakes. Egg on the top, bacon on the side, plenty of syrup. And plenty of coffee

- Before a night of action and stress, go for empty calories, fats and complex carbohydrates: pizza and soda

'His threshold of culinary acceptability was very low, but right then he felt as if he might have been pushing at the bottom edge of his personal envelope.'

**FIRST
AID**

- After giving a wounded man a shot of morphine, remember to mark his forehead with an M, to warn the medics not to give him an overdose

- When you've knocked someone unconscious, put them into the recovery position. *If* you want them to recover

'No need to put a guy in a coma over four grease marks on a shirt.'

- To set your own broken nose, smack yourself firmly in the face with the heel of your hand

- Use duct tape to keep a broken nose in place, or to patch up a knife wound

'Duct tape: the finest field dressing in the world. The Marines once flew me from the Lebanon to Germany with nothing but duct tape keeping my lower intestine in.'

- A well-aimed headbutt can leave your opponent unconscious, but may leave you with a bruised forehead

- After a fist fight, the best cure for a sore hand is to wrap it round a cold beer

>>WHAT TO DO WHEN A WOMAN FAINTS

Catch the victim

Lay her down with her feet high and her head low, so gravity helps the blood go to the brain

Check her pulse

Stimulate her with loud yells or light slaps

Persuade her to lie still for fifteen or twenty minutes

Loosen any clothing, tight or otherwise, if you think she would like you to

>>FITNESS REGIME

- Throw back the covers
- Stand up and stretch
- Arch your back
- Point your toes
- Stretch your legs

That's it

THINGS YOU'LL NEVER HEAR REACHER SAY

I need to book an appointment with my massage therapist

GETTING MAD

'I never get angry. I'm a very placid type of a guy.'

- Know when to get mad, and know when to count to ten before you get mad

'I've counted way past ten on this one. Way past.'

- Feel the aggression building, and use it and control it. Let the adrenalin pump you up

'They mess with me, they answer to me.'

- The most unbearable type of anger is a woman's – do anything to avoid it

'If they hurt her, you know what I'm going to do? I'm going to come back down here and break your spine. I'm going to stand you up and snap it like a rotten twig.'

'I wasn't angry. I was barely interested. If I had been angry, we'd be cleaning up with a fire hose. As it is we're going to need a forklift truck.'

THINGS YOU'LL NEVER HEAR REACHER SAY

Can someone help me carry my luggage?

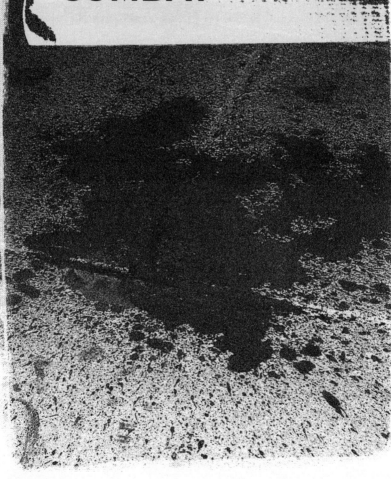

HAND-TO-HAND
COMBAT

'Fighting Reacher was like having a running chainsaw thrown at you.'

>>IN A KNIFE FIGHT

1. Don't get cut early. Nothing weakens you faster than blood loss

2. Use your fist as well as the knife. People forget you have two hands

3. It helps to be fighting for your life. And not just for fun

4. A cut to the forehead can mean so much blood it blinds your opponent

5. When someone hurts you, step in, not away

- Use whichever part of your body is the best weapon at the time

- Use your left foot if you want to mitigate the damage; calibration is an art

'Your big soft heart, Reacher. One day it will get you killed.'

- When facing an opponent with no obvious weak point, go for the eyes

'A seven-pound metal club is good. But a 250-pound human club is better.'

- Use the elbow to hit the skull; the skull is harder than the hand, the elbow gets less damaged

- When you're fighting against brass knuckles, don't get hit

- Aim for the side of the skull, which is softer and displaces the brain more

- Don't aim for the middle of the body, which is easier to defend, aim high for the head or low for the knees

- If you're swinging a weapon, get near and get near early

- If they glance up they're going to use their fists, if they glance down they're going to kick

- A headbutt changes the game. No one expects a headbutt. It's like bringing a sawn-off shotgun to a knife fight

- Basic rule of thumb with six guys: you have to be quick. You can't hit a guy less than once

'Hit them fast, hit them hard, and hit them a lot.'

THINGS YOU'LL NEVER HEAR REACHER SAY

I give up, it's hopeless

>>WAYS TO DISABLE YOUR OPPONENT

'Use a switchblade to slice the web of the guy's thumbs. Painful, and a real disincentive against holding pistols again until they have healed, which could be a long time, depending on their approach to nutrition and antisepsis.'

The best way to break a finger: wrench it sideways and snap the knuckle. Sideways is easier than bending it all the way back.

Catch a guy by the throat: do it hard enough, and fast, and numb the guy's voicebox before he can get going with any sounds. Then dig your fingers in and tap him on the top of the head, enough to send some shock down through his neck bones.

The best way to choke someone: from behind, using the thumbs on the back of the neck, and folding up the fingers so the pressure is applied from the knuckles, not the fingers, otherwise you'll get your fingers broken and your butt kicked.

'Cutting a throat doesn't take much time. Given a decent blade and enough weight and force, it takes as long as it takes to move your hand eight inches. That's all.'

HOW TO SHAKE
HANDS

1. **The combative grip.** Right at the last split second pull your hand back a fraction and close around the knuckles, not the palm. The old army trick is that they go to shake your hand, but they're aiming to crush it. A macho ritual. The way out of it is to be ready. Pull back a fraction and squeeze back. Squeeze their knuckles, not the meat of their palm. Their grip is neutralized. They never stand a chance

2. **The campaigning politician grip.** Fumble the handshake, and grip the back of the recipient's hand, not the palm, creating a breathless 'so much support here I've got to be quick' type of response. So it's strictly the shaker's choice when to let go

   Shake or squeeze. Your choice.

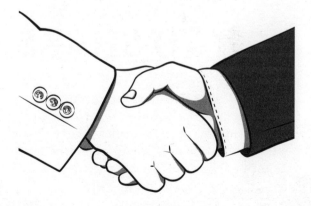

★ ★ ★ ★ ★ ★

THE WIMBLEDON CUP

WHAT

The Marine Sniper School competition, the Marine Corps 1000-yard Invitational, is the US High-Powered Long-Range Championship known as the Wimbledon Cup.

WHEN

Started in the 1870s, the competition's name may originate from the fact that the British National Rifle Association met in Wimbledon, London, in the late 19th century. It is now held in August every year.

WHERE

Camp Perry, Ohio.

WHO

The annual competition is open to shooters outside the Marines, who compete by invitation. It is a prone competition with a reputation for going to shoot-offs to decide the winner, who is regarded as the best shot in the world. Jack Reacher won the competition in 1988.

HOW

The Seven Characteristics of a Good Sniper: excellent marksman, good woodsman, emotionally stable, keenly observant, aware of his surroundings, good with a map, patient.

'It takes an awareness of the environment and total concentration at the moment you fire the shot. You have to be aware of the wind, which has a tremendous impact at 1000 yards. You have to be aware of the sun, whether it goes behind a cloud or not. Then at the last millisecond you have to develop total concentration.'

Major Jim Land, Marine Corps (retired)

'A modern army scores one enemy fatality per 15,000 rounds expended by its infantry. For specialist snipers the result is better. Way better. Twelve and a half thousand times better – a sniper scores one enemy fatality for every 1.2 rounds.'

★ ★ ★ ★ ★ ★

HITCHHIKING –
THE RULES

'Gas, grass or ass - the price of hitchhiking?'

- Set up base on a significant interchange

- Stand with one foot on the shoulder of the highway, and one in the traffic lane

- Stick out your thumb

- Stand in a way that suggests need but not desperation

- Try to look friendly (especially if you are overwhelmingly large and/or have an obvious facial wound like a broken nose)

- Smile

> *'As a mode of transportation, hitching rides was dying out. Drivers were less generous, more afraid. Because who knew what kind of a psycho you were ...'*

- Be wary of: the strong smell of weed or bourbon

- Drivers can be more compassionate at midnight than midday

- If you get a lift, give a destination. Saying 'anywhere' sounds like you're a drifter who wants to go home with them

>>WHY DRIVERS STOP TO GIVE LIFTS

1. Because people used to give *them* lifts
2. Because they're charitable and kind
3. Because they're lonely
4. Because they're so drunk they need someone else to drive the car
5. Because they think you look like their type
6. Because they've just committed a crime and need an alibi

'Hitchhiking usually carried with it the promise of random personal encounters and conversations made more intense by the certainty that their durations would necessarily be limited.'

>>HOW TO TURN A CAR OVER

Let the tyres and suspension do the work.

Rock the car hard. Then bounce it until it's coming up for air at about 45 degrees.

Hook hands under the sill and heave the car all the way onto its side.

Then keep the momentum going and tip it onto its roof.

HOW TO
EXTRACT
INFORMATION

'It's all about free will. It's all about making choices. You can tell me now, or you can tell me after I break your legs.'

- The hardest part of any adversarial conversation is the beginning. An early answer is a good sign. Answering becomes a habit

- Ask once, ask twice if you must, but don't ask three times

- First chat about shared interests to build up trust, then it's harder for them to start lying

'Be sceptical, but not too sceptical. Too much scepticism leads to paranoia and paralysis.'

- If the night shift won't help you, maybe the day shift will. (Night workers are always tougher – less contact with the public)

- Ask a librarian – they're nice people, they tell you things if you ask them

*'Three can keep a secret, if two of
them are dead.'*

Benjamin Franklin

- Only resort to threatening physical violence as a last resort

**'Either you walk out of here by yourself, or
you'll be carried out in a bucket.'**

KNOW HOW TO FIND YOUR WAY AROUND A CITY

'Every city has a cusp, where the good part of town turns bad.'

FINDING AN AUTOPARTS STORE
In any city the autoparts store is always on the same strip as the tyre stores and the auto dealers and the lube shops. Which in any city is always a wide new strip near a highway clover-leaf.

FINDING THE MORGUE
Morgues are usually close to hospitals, well hidden from the public. They are often not signposted at all, or else labelled something anodyne like Special Services. But they're always accessible. Meat wagons have to be able to roll in and out unobstructed.

FINDING THE SHERIFF'S OFFICE
Turn off the main drag – public offices are always in
the back somewhere where land is cheaper – and
check the side streets. Look for a shortwave antenna
on the roof and a lot big enough for a handful of
cruisers.

FINDING A WESTERN UNION OFFICE
Stand on a street corner and ask yourself, is it more
likely to be left or right now? Then turn left or right as
appropriate, and pretty soon you are in the right
neighbourhood, and pretty soon you find it.
If in doubt, turn left.

'The bad stuff seems to migrate. Law enforcement never really wins. It just shoves stuff around, a block here, a block there.'

★ ★ ★ ★ ★ ★

WEST POINT

WHAT

Established in 1802, the United States Military Academy at West Point educates and trains around a thousand select cadets every year to become officers. After four years, most graduates leave with a commission as second lieutenant.

WHERE

Fifty miles north of New York City, the academy campus occupies 16,000 acres on a commanding plateau on the west bank of the Hudson River.

WHO

Applicants must have an above-average academic record, qualities of leadership and be fit, strong and agile. They are nominated either by a person connected with the service or by a member of congress.

Officers making simple shit hard since 1802

THE WEST POINT MISSION
'To educate, train, and inspire the Corps of Cadets so that each graduate is a commissioned leader of character committed to the values of Duty, Honor, Country and prepared for a career of professional excellence and service to the Nation as an officer in the United States Army.'

Old West Point saying:

Everybody has a plan until they get punched in the mouth.

KEEP ON
THE MOVE

> *'Everyone's life needs an organizing principle, and relentless forward motion was Reacher's.'*

- Always move on and never look back. Never do the same thing twice

- The best place for a nomad to sleep is a motel. It has beds and doors that lock. Pay cash and don't give your real name

'Part of being a drifter means you look forward, not backward. You concentrate on what's ahead.'

- Arrange the smallest details in your life so that you can move on at a split second's notice

- Own nothing, carry nothing

- Two days in one place is about the limit

'Mostly he had rocked and swayed and dozed on buses, watching the passing scenes, observing the chaos of America, and surfing along on memories. His life was like that.'

'I'm a nomad.'
'Nomads have animals. They move around to find pasture. That's the definition.'
'OK, I'm a nomad without the animal part.'

- Transience is a habit you can't break

- A wad of dollars means ... a few more weeks when you don't have to find a job

- Don't do permanent, be a Reacher, not a Settler

- Take the first bus out

'They say you need to ride the rails for a while to understand the travelling blues. They're wrong. To understand the travelling blues you need to be locked down somewhere. In a cell. Or in the army. Someplace where you're caged. Someplace where smokestack lightning looks like a far-away beacon of impossible freedom.'

CODES USED BY THE MILITARY POLICE

10–2 Ambulance urgently needed

10–3 Motor vehicle accident

10–4 Wrecker requested

10–7 Pick up prisoner

10–8 Subject in custody

10–9 Send police van

10–10 Escort/transport

10–13 Repeat last message

10–14 Your location?

10–15 Go to …

10–16 Contact by secure landline

10–17 Return to base

10–18 Assignment completed/mission accomplished

10–19 Contact by phone or radio

10–22 Fire

10–23 Disturbance

10–24 Suspicious person

10–25 Stolen/abandoned vehicle

10–26 Serious accident

10–28 Loud and clear

10–29 Weak signal

10–30 Need assistance

10–31 Request investigator

10–32 Request MP duty officer

10–33 Stand by

10–34 Cancel last message

10–35 Meal

10–36 Please forward my messages

10–62 Fellow officer in trouble, requests urgent assistance

Or use the secret Alphabet Code, as in:

'We'd rate him SAS, sir.' (Stupid Asshole Sometimes)

LESSONS
LEARNED IN
THE MILITARY

- Hurry up and wait

'Hurry up and wait was the real MP motto. Not *Assist, Protect, Defend.*'

- Never volunteer for anything. Soldier's basic rule

- Confusion and unpredictability are what you should expect

- If in doubt, be flippant

- When the navy says three hours, it means three hours. One hundred and eighty minutes, not a second more, not a second less

- The soldierly way to kill people is to shoot or stab or hit or strangle. They don't do subtle

- Confront your enemies

'Back in the day.'

'Delta is full of guys who can stay awake for a week and walk a hundred miles and shoot the balls off a tsetse fly, but it's relatively empty of guys who can do all that and then tell you the difference between a Shiite and a trip to the latrines.'

- Almost any place is serviceable – there is always somewhere worse to compare it with

- First you check, then you double-check

- Eat every time you can, sleep every time you can

>>TWO WAYS TO GET PROMOTED

1. Let them think you're just a little dumber than they are
2. Raise a glass to 'bloody wars and dread diseases'

- If in doubt, go formal

- Preconceptions get in the way

'With manpower like the army has, you can find a needle in a haystack. You can find both halves of the broken needle. You can find the tiny chip of chrome that flaked off the break.'

- In the army you learn how to sleep anywhere, anytime

- Initiative in the ranks usually ends in tears. Especially when live ammunition is involved

- The military and civilians will always remain a mystery to each other

> *'I guess I don't understand the military.'*
> *'Well, don't feel bad about it. We don't understand you either.'*

LIVE OFF
THE GRID

'He was pretty sure he didn't want to live in a house. The desire just passed him by. The necessary involvement intimidated him. It was a physical weight, exactly like the suitcase in his hand.'

- Don't own a house. You could be traced by paying property tax, insurance, electricity, heating, water... even the electoral roll

- If you never rent an apartment, or even a room, they'll never be able to trace you by your last known address

'You're the only person I know who *wants* to be homeless.'

- Don't own a car. You have to pay insurance, oil changes, inspection, tax, gasoline. You'll be identified by your car's registration number. Hitch a ride, or hop on a Greyhound bus

'He knew people with houses. He had talked to them, with the same kind of detached interest he would talk to a person who kept snakes as pets or entered ballroom dancing competitions.'

- Don't use a phone. Especially a smartphone. And especially not one with GPS to give away your location

- Don't use a credit card, use cash

- Use aliases for checking into motels

'Now they broke my toothbrush I don't own anything.'

HOGAN'S ALLEY

WHAT
Where new FBI and DEA agents train to deal with mobsters, terrorists and gunfights in a realistic simulated urban setting.

Built with the help of Hollywood set designers, it has a post office, the All-Med Pharmacy, a hotel, the Hogan Bank, a laundromat, a barber's shop the Dogwood Inn, several town houses, and the Biograph Theater.

WHERE
Occupies 10 acres at the FBI training academy in Quantico, Virginia.

HOW
In simulated hand-to-hand combat, shoot-outs, bank robberies, kidnapping, assaults and carjacking, the trainee agents learn arrest procedures, street survival techniques and control holds.

'We don't teach them to fight fair, and we don't start a fight.'

ON WALKING THROUGH A THIRTY-INCH DOORWAY

THE BEST PLACES TO LOOK
FOR A CAREFULLY HiDDEN KEY

- VCR slot
- Kettle
- Shoe
- Inside a TV set
- Battery compartment
  of a transistor radio
- Hollowed-out book

- Foam of the inside of
  a car seat
- Tub of cream cheese
- Toilet tank
- Mattress
- Under loose floorboards
- Hot stove

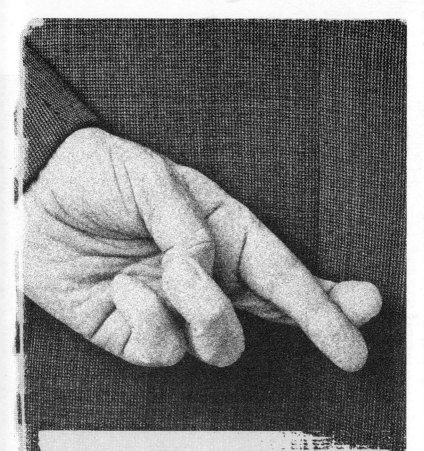

HOW TO TELL IF
THEY'RE LYING

☞ A liar usually has all the signs on display: gulps, false starts, stammers and fidgets.

☞ The memory centre is in the left brain, the imagination in the right – so a glance to the left generally means they're remembering things, to the right they're making stuff up.

☞ They'll avoid eye contact, and touch or scratch their nose or ear.

☞ A truthful person is perfectly capable of saying no, but generally they stop and think about it first. The one who says no immediately is usually lying.

'I can lie with the best of them ... sadly.'

LEARN TO READ THEIR BODY LANGUAGE

Q: Is he adjusting a cuff or watchstrap with his arm across his body?

A: *He feels nervous and may have something to hide.*

Q: Is he unconsciously covering his genitals?

A: *He feels insecure in your company.*

Q: Is she sitting with her legs crossed, dangling a shoe that is pointing at you?

A: *She's interested.*

Q: Is he standing with his legs wide apart?

A: *He's getting ready to punch you.*

MAN WALKS INTO A BAR –
THE RULES

'For a military cop, going into a bar is like a batter stepping up to the plate. It's his place of business.'

1. Count the exits (there are usually three)

2. Work out which exits you can use

3. Look at the crowd – where are the knots of trouble, who falls silent, who stares

4. Look for weapons – antique revolvers, bottles, or – better – pool cues

5. Stare everyone down

6. Sit with your back to the wall, even if there are plenty of mirrors

7. Call 911 – the other guys are going to need an ambulance …

'It was a long, long time since he'd lost a two-on-one bar fight.'

A MEDLEY OF MILITARY ACRONYMS

ACU Army Combat Uniform

ALICE All-Purpose Lightweight Carrying Equipment

APFSDS Armour Piercing Fin Stabilized Discarding Sabot

ATF Bureau of Alcohol, Tobacco and Firearms

BDU Battle Dress Uniform

COS Chief of Staff

CYA Cover Your Ass

DEA Drug Enforcement Administration

DIA Defense Intelligence Agency

DOD Department of Defense

HET Heavy Equipment Transporter

HRT Hostage Rescue Team

JAG Judge Advocate General

KIA Killed In Action

LAV Light Armored Vehicle

LGH Let's Go Home

MASH Mobile Army Surgical Hospital

MPBN Military Police Battalion

MIA Missing In Action

MRE Meal Ready to Eat

NCIC National Crime Information Center

PASGT Personal Armor System, Ground Troops

PH Public House

RIF Reduction In Force

RPG Rocket Propelled Grenade

RTAFA Rotational Torque-Adjustable Fastener Applicators

SAC Special Agent in Charge

SEAL Sea Air and Land (US Navy SEALs)

SOC Special Operations Capable

SOP Standard Operating Procedure

SSDD Same Shit Different Day

SWAG Scientific Wild-Ass Guess

UNSUB Unknown Subject

USA PATRIOT ACT Uniting and Strengthening America by Providing Appropriate Tools Required to Intercept and Obstruct Terrorism Act

WTF Whisky Tango Foxtrot …

RESPECT YOUR OPPONENT

'Dealing with morons … is like teaching Hindu to a beagle.'

'He was in no imminent danger of winning the Nobel Prize, but definitely smarter than the average bear.'

'He wasn't the crispest shirt in the closet.'

' "You're pretty good for an old guy." "That's how I got to be an old guy," McGrath said.'

'You have a message? Who from? The National Association of Assholes?'

'He'd fallen out of the ugly tree and hit every branch.'

'I nodded amiably at the two of them. I figured they had less than an hour to live.'

'Guys like these, they couldn't find their own assholes if I gave them a mirror on a stick.'

NOTICING
STUFF

'He was an observant man. He had made his living by noticing details. He was *living* because he noticed details.'

- Think about everything you've seen and heard. Work the clues

>>KNOW THE SIGNS OF BEING UNDER SURVEILLANCE

- unexplained cars
- parked vans
- pairs or trios of dressed-down people with wires in their ears
- clean taxi cabs with two people in them
- pedestrians you see inexplicably in two different places

- The width of a person's wrists is the best indicator of their strength

- People don't like searching above head height. If you want to hide something, hide it on the top shelf

- People hiding and waiting give off human vibrations. If you don't feel them they're not there

- An elected official always has a separate brass plate. (It makes it cheaper when the guy changes every few Novembers)

- The easiest way to spot a hooker is by their big purse – they have to carry around a lot of stuff (condoms, massage oils, gun, credit card machine ...)

- If a lock doesn't have scratches around it then no one uses the door

'I think Reacher's the kind of guy that sees things five seconds before the rest of the world.'

- Look, don't see, listen, don't hear. The more you engage, the longer you survive

- If somebody's got money outside of their salary, it shows up somewhere

'Suicide bombers give out all kinds of tell-tale signs. Mostly because they're nervous. By definition they're all first-timers.'

>>THE PERFECT OBSERVATION POINT

A soldier knows that the perfect observation point provides:

1. An unobstructed view to the front

2. Adequate security to the flanks and rear

3. Protection from the elements

4. Concealment of observers

5. A reasonable likelihood of undisturbed occupation

6. A result

THE TWELVE SIGNS OF A SUICIDE BOMBER

(as identified by Israeli counterintelligence)

- -

1. Inappropriate clothing – oversized or padded coat

2. A robotic walk – because of carrying unaccustomed weight

3. Irritability

4. Sweating

5. Tics

6. Nervous behaviour

7. Low and controlled breathing, panting

8. Staring rigidly ahead

9. Mumbled prayers

10. A large bag

11. Hands in the bag

12. A lack of suntan from a fresh shave (male), lack of suntan from taking off a headscarf (female)

The US Army Military Police

CODE OF ETHICS

I AM A SOLDIER IN THE UNITED STATES ARMY.

I AM OF THE TROOPS AND FOR THE TROOPS.

I HOLD ALLEGIANCE TO MY COUNTRY AND DEVOTION TO DUTY ABOVE ALL ELSE.

I PROUDLY RECOGNIZE MY OBLIGATION TO PERFORM MY DUTY WITH INTEGRITY, LOYALTY, AND HONESTY.

I WILL ASSIST AND PROTECT MY FELLOW SOLDIERS IN A MANNER THAT IS FAIR, COURTEOUS, AND IMPARTIAL.

I WILL PROMOTE, BY PERSONAL EXAMPLE, THE HIGHEST STANDARDS OF SOLDIERING, STRESSING PERFORMANCE AND PROFESSIONALISM.

I WILL STRIVE TO MERIT THE RESPECT OF OTHERS; SEEKING NO FAVOR BECAUSE OF POSITION BUT INSTEAD, THE SATISFACTION OF A MISSION ACCOMPLISHED AND A JOB WELL DONE.

★ ★ ★ ★ ★ ★

And

I DO NOT MESS WITH THE SPECIAL INVESTIGATORS

REACHER'S MORAL CODE

'I don't want to put the world to rights, I just don't like people who put the world to wrongs.'

✪ You reap what you sow.

'I have to warn you. I promised my mother, a long time ago. She said I had to give folks a chance to walk away.'

✪ Don't do what the law says, do what's right.

'You don't start fights but you sure as hell finish them, and you don't lose them either.'

✪ Never forgive, never forget.

✪ You are only accountable to your own conscience.

✪ Do it once and do it right.

'I try to do the right things. I think the reasons don't really matter. I like to see the right thing done.'

'With a better attitude he could have been Chief of Staff by now.'

'We investigate, we prepare, we execute. We find them, we take them down.'

Military Police

TRAINING

US military policemen are trained to maintain order, investigate crimes, and offer security in combat zones.

Training takes place for nine weeks at Fort Leonard Wood's Stem Village, an imitation town complete with houses, jail, a bank and a theatre. Recruits are taught skills including marksmanship, unarmed combat, investigation, VIP protection, evasive driving, surveillance and First Aid; and how to deal with sabotage, suicide, damage to private property, and dead bodies. They also study Miranda rights, military law, collecting evidence, search and apprehension, interrogation, and directing traffic.

It's not about strength or violence, but all about technique, making the right moves and striking in the right places – to physically restrain a perpetrator.

★ ★ ★ ★ ★ ★

NEVER OFF DUTY

HOW TO OPEN A LOCKED IRON GATE WITH A CHRYSLER

----

1. Open all the windows of the car to lessen the noise, so that the bang on impact doesn't deafen you completely.

2. Hold up one arm in front of you to stop yourself being knocked out by the airbag.

3. Position the car about fifteen feet from the gate.

4. Rev the engine to the maximum with your foot on the brake until the car is rocking and straining.

5. Suddenly release brake and stamp on the accelerator, shoot forward and smash the gate.

6. Get the hell out of there before the cops turn up.

THE SCIENCE OF ... THE PERFECT SHOT

The perfect bullet

... has to be a perfect little artefact. It's got to be as good as any manufactured article has ever been. It has got to be cast better than any jewellery. It must be totally uniform in size and weight. Perfectly round, perfectly streamlined. It has to accept ferocious rotation from the rifling grooves inside the barrel. It has to spin and hiss through the air with absolutely no wobble, no bias.

The perfect barrel

... has to be tight and straight. No good at all if a previous shot has heated and altered the barrel shape. The barrel has to be a mass of perfect metal, heavy enough to remain inert. Heavy enough to kill the tiny vibrations of the bolt and the trigger and the firing pin.

The perfect powder

… behind the bullet in the shell case has to explode perfectly, predictably, powerfully, instantly. It has to smash the projectile down the barrel at maximum speed. The powder has to explode fast, explode completely, and explode hard. Difficult chemistry. Weight for weight, that explosion has got to be the best explosion on the planet.

The perfect shot

LAUND[

**PERSONAL
GROOMING**

'He glanced at himself in an old spotted mirror. Six-five, two-fifty, hands as big as frozen turkeys, hair all over the place, unshaven, torn shirt cuffs up on his forearms like Frankenstein's monster. A bum.'

1. ALWAYS SHAVE AND GET A GOOD HAIRCUT

A whitewall. Leave an inch and a half on the top and use clippers to shave the bottom and the sides up towards it. Then flip the clippers over and square off the sideburns and clean the fuzz off the neck. Unless you're going undercover.

2. DON'T SKIP THE SHOWER

Four kinds, depending on circumstances:

a. The straight shower (11 minutes) – shower and hairwash

b. The shave and shower (22 minutes) – shave, hairwash, shower

c. The special procedure (30 minutes +) – shower and hairwash, shave, shower and second hairwash

d. The even longer one. When you've got company

'He knew he was out of step with the western world in terms of how often he changed his clothes, but he tried to compensate by keeping his body scrupulously clean.'

3. ALWAYS CARRY A TOOTHBRUSH

Even for a man without luggage, it's essential to have your own toothbrush, preferably a folding one that you can keep in your pocket. In the absence of toothpaste, freshen your mouth with gum.

If you can't get time to sleep, a shower is a good substitute. If you can't get time to shower, cleaning your teeth is the next best thing.

*'His folding toothbrush was on the
floor, stepped on and crushed.
"Bastards," he said.'*

4. HOW TO KEEP CLOTHES CLEAN ON THE ROAD

Option 1 – after every three to four days soak or
rinse clothes and place under mattress to press.

Option 2 – after up to nine days put clothes in trash
and buy a new set.

Option 3 – if you dress in wet clothes you've got a
built-in air conditioner that keeps you cool while
they dry out.

*'He folded his pants and his shirt
very carefully and put them flat
under the mattress. That was as
close as ever he got to ironing.'*

THINGS YOU'LL NEVER SEE REACHER DO

Take a suit to the dry cleaner's

'A good coat is like a good lawyer. It covers your ass.'

5. CHANGING YOUR UNDERWEAR

- Always buy the cheapest white underpants

- Remember that khaki socks will give you away if you're going undercover

- Most people stick to underwear from their country of origin. It's a big step putting on foreign underwear, like betrayal or emigration

- If caught short, go commando

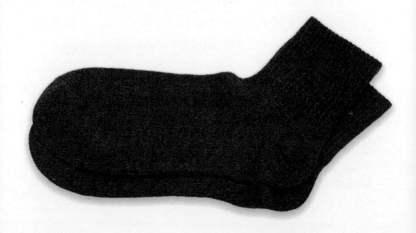

>>THE LONGEST TIME A TRAVELLING MAN CAN GO WITHOUT...

A shower	4 days
Changing his clothes	9 days
Changing his underwear	9 days

THINGS YOU'LL NEVER HEAR REACHER SAY

My wife doesn't understand me

THE PENTAGON

★　★　★　★　★　★

WHAT
Headquarters of the US Department of Defense. Completed in January 1943, it covers 600,000 square metres of floor area – the world's largest office building. About 31,000 military and civilian employees work there. It has five rings of corridor per floor on five floors – covering seventeen miles. There is a five-acre pentagonal courtyard in the middle.

WHERE
Arlington County, Virginia, on the Potomac River flood plain.

HOW
Departments within the DOD control the army, navy, air force, military technology, budget, and policy.

HOW FAST
There are ten radial hallways between the rings; travelling at army marching pace of 4mph, a person can make it between any two random points inside a maximum seven minutes.

'To escape into the Pentagon was no kind of a good idea.'

**Q: What happens more than 250 times a day
in the Pentagon?**

A: A light bulb is changed.

WHY IT'S NOT SMART TO HAVE A PHONE

'I'm that guy ... The only guy in the world who doesn't have a cell phone.'

- Remember that if the satellite can show you the way on your GPS, it can also pinpoint your exact location

- The guy who relies on his head clock has no use for a fancy watch

'He came from a world where a sudden dive for a pocket was more likely to mean a gun than a phone.'

- Put your brain first – electronic devices can affect your ability to process information, your concentration, and your sleep

- Why would you want to allow the world and his wife to track you down by phone?

- If you're constantly looking down at your phone, you're not looking at the world around you

'Text messaging.'

'What's that?'

'You can send written messages by phone.'

'When did that start?'

THINGS YOU'LL NEVER HEAR REACHER SAY

Call me on my cell

POTENTIAL ALIASES FOR USE WHEN BOOKING A MOTEL

'It helps if you can use a list of names embedded in your memory. Like the US Presidents.'

GUESTS

George Washington, John Adams, Thomas Jefferson, James Madison, James Monroe, John Quincy Adams, Andrew Jackson, Martin Van Buren, William H. Harrison, John Tyler, James K. Polk, Zachary Taylor, Millard Fillmore, Franklin Pierce, James Buchanan, Abraham Lincoln, Andrew Johnson, Ulysses S. Grant, Rutherford B. Hayes, James A. Garfield, Chester A. Arthur, Grover Cleveland, Benjamin Harrison, William McKinley, Theodore Roosevelt, William H. Taft, Woodrow Wilson, Warren G. Harding, Calvin Coolidge, Herbert Hoover

'If in doubt, use the names of obscure baseball players, or dead musicians.'

'I like aliases. I like anonymity.'

USE YOUR WITS
- PSYCHOLOGY

'I don't need to go hunting them. I already know I'm smarter than an armadillo.'

- The basis of any scam is telling people what they want to hear. If something sounds too good to be true, it probably is

- A classic confidence trick is where you drip, drip, drip the unimportant stuff but then hold back on the final instalment

- Assess and evaluate

- Paranoia prefers triple bluffs to double bluffs

- Killers don't stop at two murders. If they do more than one, they do more than two

'People don't look for complications. You hear hoofbeats, you look for horses, not zebras.'

'Something for nothing, that's a foreign language.'

- All good scam artists stick as close to the truth as possible

- There's always something out of context, even before you know what the context ought to be

- Force yourself to think like they think

'The whole of life is a gamble, from the very beginning to the very end.'

MIRANDA

The Miranda warning is used by US police when questioning criminal suspects, to protect the individual from compelled self-incrimination, and to preserve the admissibility of their statement in court. It originated in 1966 after *Miranda vs Arizona*, when an Ernesto Arturo Miranda was deemed to have had his rights violated during his arrest.

- **You have the right to remain silent**

- **Anything you say or do can and will be held against you in a court of law**

- **You have the right to speak to an attorney**

- **If you cannot afford an attorney, one will be appointed for you**

- **Do you understand these rights as they have been read to you?**

'"Ernesto A. Miranda was a moron, you know that?" Deerfield said. "A couple of smokes short of a pack. He was a subnormal guy. He needed the protection. You subnormal? You a moron, Reacher?"

"Probably, to be putting up with this shit."'

THE SCIENCE OF ...
BURNING DOWN A BUILDING

- Place books of matches under furniture in the centre of the room

- Pile as much paper as you can find on top, lean a burning cigarette against the matches

- Retire, leaving the door open for a draught

Brick buildings always burn well. The contents go up first, then the floors, ceiling and roof with the outer walls holding up and forming a tall chimney to enhance the air flow. When the walls finally collapse, the blast of sparks and embers will spread the fire further.

Sometimes a whole city block can be taken out with one cigarette and one book of matches.

SLEEP

'I'm sleeping well ... but I think that's mostly because of the tranquillizers.'

- Sleep when you can, because you never know when you're going to sleep again

- Accept that you'll never find a bed that will accommodate your feet as well as your head

- Careful, sleep can be a symptom of caffeine deprivation

- Sleep as much as you can because tiredness causes more foul-ups than carelessness and stupidity put together

- If you go to sleep fully dressed, you'll be ready for action when you wake

- You'll feel safer sleeping with a handgun under your pillow

'A medical man would say I passed out. I prefer to think I just went to sleep.'

KNOWING THE
TIME

*'He set the clock in his head for two
hours, and he breathed in once,
and he breathed out once, and then
he fell asleep, almost instantly.'*

Tune into your circadian rhythms to set your personal
internal alarm clock.

Four o'clock in the morning is the best time to attack.
In the Army they call it KGB time.

*'Clocks in prisons are bizarre. Why
measure hours and minutes when
people think in years and decades?'*

THINGS YOU'LL NEVER HEAR REACHER SAY

Any idea what the time is?

'He knew what time it was to within about twenty seconds. It was an old skill, born of many long wakeful nights on active service.

When you're waiting for something to happen, you close your body down like a beach house in winter and you let your mind lock on to the steady pace of the passing seconds. It's like suspended animation. It saves energy and it lifts the responsibility for your heartbeat away from your unconscious brain and passes it on to some kind of a hidden clock. Makes a huge black space for thinking in.

But it keeps you just awake enough to be ready for whatever you need to be ready for.

And it means you always know what time it is.'

TRAVEL
LIGHT

'I've got no use for possessions. Travel light, travel far.'

- Never carry a spare shirt

- Be on as few pieces of paper as it is possible for a human being to be

'To fill a small bag means selecting, and choosing, and evaluating. Pretty soon I'd have a big bag, and then two or three. A month later I'd be like the rest of you.'

- Never have a credit card, real estate, a driver's licence, a car, a wife, children, or an address

- Take one day at a time

'I'm not a vagrant ... I'm a hobo. Big difference.'

- Always travel by road – you don't need ID and can pay with cash

'Carry a spare shirt and pretty soon you're carrying spare pants. Then you need a suitcase. Next thing you know, you've got a house and a car and a savings plan and you're filling out all kinds of forms.'

THINGS YOU'LL NEVER SEE REACHER DO

Buy a business-class airline ticket

WHAT TO DO IN THE FACE OF:

STUPIDITY

MISUNDERSTANDING

IMPERTINENT PERSONAL
QUESTIONS

EMPTY THREATS

BAD GUYS WHO WON'T TAKE
THE HINT AND BACK OFF

Shrug

WHEN TO
SPEAK

'Reacher said nothing.'

- If in doubt, say nothing

- Keeping your mouth shut is a devastating weapon

- Your silence will make your opponent want to babble

- Say nothing, do nothing

- You need a reason for speech, but you need more for silence

'Reacher made no reply. It was a technique he had perfected half a lifetime ago. Just stand absolutely still, don't blink, say nothing. Wait for them to run through the possibilities. Wait for them to start worrying.'

BLIND BLAKE

(Right) The only known photograph of Blind Blake, whose life – and death – remain something of a mystery.

Born Arthur Blake in 1896 in (probably) Jacksonville, Florida, Blind Blake's distinctive guitar playing sounded like a ragtime piano. Blind from birth, he is still regarded as the unrivalled master of ragtime blues finger-picking, who could play a complete band arrangement by himself. Between 1926 and 1932 he recorded over eighty tracks for Paramount, which were big sellers in their day. After Paramount's bankruptcy Blake became a heavy drinker and died, by accident or disease, at the age of thirty-eight. But there is also a story that he was murdered in Margrave, Georgia.

'You know that old expression he could play the guitar just like ringing a bell? That's what I used to say about Blake. He would pick up that old instrument of his and the notes would just come tumbling out, faster than you could sing them. But each note was just a perfect little silver bell, floating off into the air.'

HOW TO WIN
THE BATTLE

'For the infantry it all came down to simple arithmetic. If you could inflict two casualties for every one you took, you were ahead.'

'To fail to take the battle to the enemy when your back is to the wall is to perish.'

Sun Tzu, *The Art of War*

- Think like the enemy, *be* the enemy

- When contemplating the offensive, the first thing you must plan is your inevitable retreat

- If your attack is going too well, you have walked into an ambush

- Combat will occur on the ground between two adjoining maps

- Never leave enemy ordnance usable

'All plans fall apart as soon as the first shot is fired.'

- Friendly fire isn't that friendly

- If you can't attack at one end, you have to defend at the other

- Incoming fire has the right of way

- Double back to positions the enemy think are abandoned

- If you're surrounded, that simplifies your problems

'A good battle plan that you act on today can be better than a perfect one tomorrow.'

Gen. George S. Patten

HOW TO WIN
THE WAR

'Sooner or later, you've got to engage the enemy's main force. You don't win the war unless you do that. You take it on and you destroy it.'

- In order to win, you must be prepared to lose

- Don't worry about why it went wrong. Just damn well put it right

- Know how to deceive the enemy, and that sooner or later they have to be fought head on

- If you attack you have to keep on and on attacking until the enemy is run off its feet and the war is won

- Everything in war is improvisation

- Try to look unimportant. They may be low on ammo

- Never retreat, just advance in the opposite direction

'While coolness in disaster is the supreme proof of a commander's courage, energy in pursuit is the surest test of his strength of will.'

Field Marshal Viscount Wavell

'They mess with me, they answer to me.'

'War isn't about dying for your country. It's about making the enemy die for his.'

Gen. George S. Patten

MAN'S TOYS

'Cocked and locked.'

1 Beretta M9 Over two decades of distinguished service in the US Army

2 Glock 17 Extremely simple and extremely reliable

3 Heckler & Koch MP5K A submachine gun for law enforcement

4 M-16 assault rifle For a long time the US Army's weapon of choice

5 SIG-Sauer P226 Swiss excellence

6 Smith & Wesson Military and Police revolver Old-fashioned excellence

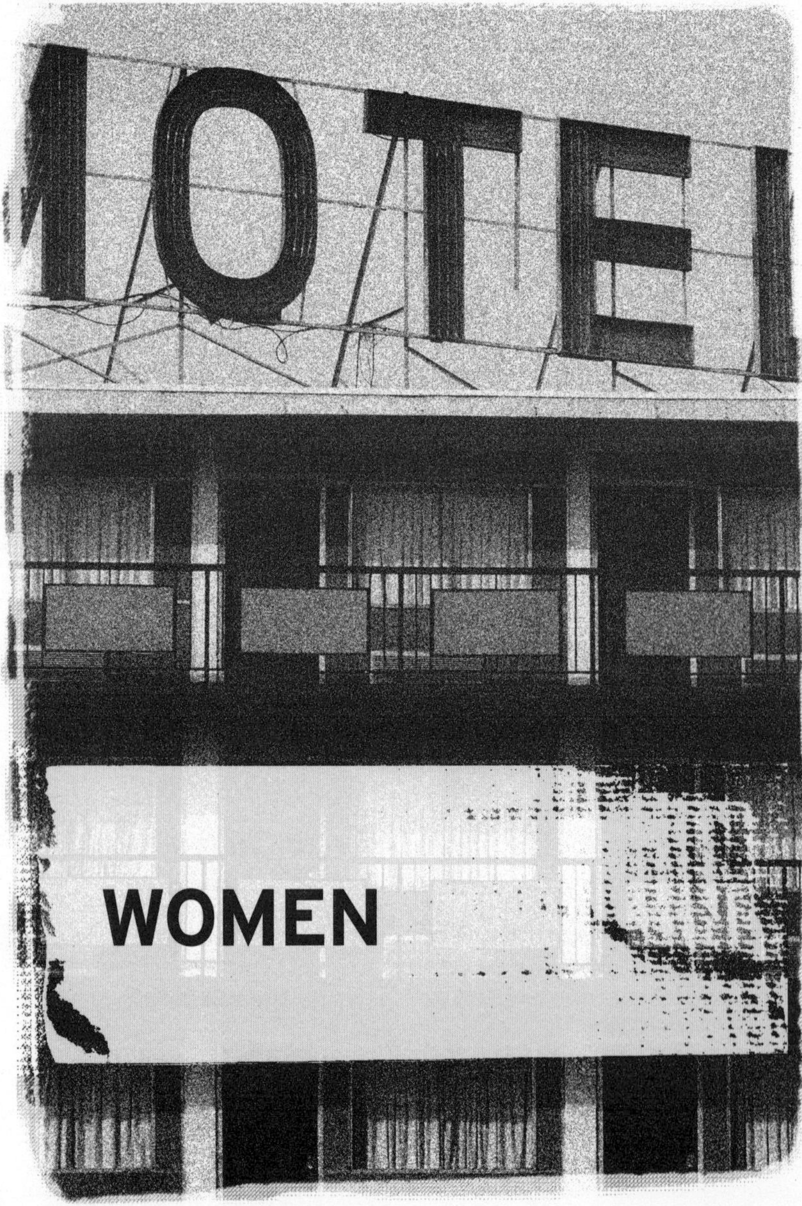

WOMEN

'If you really want to know, one at a time is usually enough for me.'

A brave girl is one who stands up when she hears gunshots. She doesn't dive under the desk.

Show a woman respect, and she's yours.

Undressing a woman is one of life's greatest perks. Especially Lycra – can't beat it.

'He smiled. "I was thinking about your dress."

"You like it?"

"I think it's great," he said. "But it could look better. You know, maybe thrown in a heap on the floor."'

'I like women in uniform, possibly because I've known very few of the other kind.'

There's nothing shameful about taking orders from a woman of superior rank.

Only have one affair at a time – that's complicated enough.

'I don't do permanent.'

Older women ... are worth it.

Female police officers carry handcuffs, which can be handy in bed.

Accept no as an answer, if she's crazy enough to turn you down.

'She was more than flawless. She was spectacular. She had a revolver in a holster on her right hip, and next to it was a shotgun stuffed muzzle-down in a scabbard mounted between the seats.'

'You like undressing women?'

*'More than anything in the world,'
I said. 'And I've been staring at that
particular button since a quarter
past nine.'*

If you can stand to watch her eat, that has to mean something.

Never hit a woman unless she's trying to kill you.

Never make love in a car – they're not usually wide enough.

If you're guessing a woman's age, always err on the side of caution and knock off a couple of years.

Only very experienced men should try to guess a woman's bra size by her voice.

Love them and leave them.

'Your ass deserves nothing but the best. It's a national treasure. Or a regional attraction at the very least.'

THINGS YOU'LL NEVER HEAR REACHER SAY

Hey, babe, your place or mine?

HOW TO SLEEP
IN A $350-A-NIGHT
HOTEL
ROOM FOR $50

★ ★ ★ ★ ★

Start late, around midnight

Ask the night clerk for an
available room

Tell him you need to
check it out

Get him to come with you

Once you're in it, offer him
two twenties

And ten for the maid

He's happy

You've got a cheap room
for the night

HOW TO
LEAVE TOWN

FIND

the road out of town,
stand by the side of it,
and stick out your thumb.

OR:

FIND

the bus station
and get on the first bus out.

DON'T

look back.

For details of Jack Reacher's
adventures and books
by Lee Child, go to
www.leechild.com.